Fall Harvest

by

Gail Saunders-Smith

Pebble Books

an imprint of Capstone Press

Pebble Books

Pebble Books are published by Capstone Press
818 North Willow Street, Mankato, Minnesota 56001
http://www.capstone-press.com
Copyright © 1998 by Capstone Press

Library of Congress Cataloging-in-Publication Data
Saunders-Smith, Gail.
 Fall harvest/by Gail Saunders-Smith.
  p. cm.
 Includes bibliographical references (p. 23) and index.
 Summary: Simple text and photographs describe how several
different crops, including pumpkins, apples, wheat, corn, and
potatoes, are harvested by humans and by machine.
 ISBN 1-56065-587-9
 1. Harvesting--Juvenile literature. 2. Food crops--
Harvesting--Juvenile literature. [1. Food crops--Harvesting.
2. Harvesting.] I. Title.

SB129.S38 1998
631.5'5--dc21   97-29800
                                  CIP
                                  AC

Editorial Credits
Lois Wallentine, editor; Timothy Halldin and James Franklin,
design; Michelle L. Norstad, photo research

Photo Credits
Chuck Haney, 18
Kay Shaw, 10
John Marshall, 14
Unicorn Stock/Alice Prescott, cover; Martha McBride, 6; Dennis
 MacDonald, 1, 8; Doris Brookes, 12; Herbert L. Stormont, 16;
 Kimberly Burnham, 20
Willowbrook Photography/Ken Weidenbach, 4

Table of Contents

4

In the fall, people pick pumpkins.

People pick apples.

Machines harvest wheat.

10

Machines harvest sugar beets.

People pick potatoes.

Machines harvest potatoes, too.

People pick corn.

Machines harvest corn, too.

Both people and machines harvest cranberries in the fall.

Words to Know

apple—a round, crisp fruit that grows on a tree

corn—the seeds produced on a tall grass plant; the seeds grow in rows within a pod that is called an ear; people eat these seeds as a vegetable

cranberry—a small, red, tart berry that grows on small bushes in wet ground

harvest—to gather crops

potato—a round or oblong vegetable that grows underground

pumpkin—a large, round, orange fruit that grows on a vine

sugar beet—a vegetable that grows underground, which is used to make sugar

wheat—the seeds produced on a certain type of grass; the seeds are used to make flour, pasta, and breakfast foods

Read More

Bryant-Mole, Karen. *Autumn.* Crystal Lake, Ill.: Rigby Interactive Library, 1997.

Hutchings, Amy and Richard Hutchings. *Picking Apples and Pumpkins.* New York: Scholastic, Inc., 1994.

My First Look at Seasons. New York: Random House, 1990.

Internet Sites

Dept of Ag Kids' Page
http://www.state.il.us/agr/kidspage

The Maize Page
http://www.ag.iastate.edu/departments/agronomy/cornpage.html

Seeds of Change Garden
http://horizon.nmsu.edu/garden

Note to Parents and Teachers

This book illustrates and describes the types of foods that are harvested in the fall and how they are harvested. The text and photographs enable young children to see and understand where our food comes from. The clear photographs support the beginning reader in making and maintaining the meaning of the text. Children may need assistance in using the Table of Contents, Words to Know, Read More, Internet Sites, and Index/Word List sections of the book.

Index/Word List

Word Count: 39